stiles

FABRIC
Photo
Play

Love to Quilt...

Julia C. Wood

Located in Paducah, Kentucky, the American Quilter's Society (AQS) is dedicated to promoting the accomplishments of today's quilters. Through its publications and events, AQS strives to honor today's quiltmakers and their work and to inspire future creativity and innovation in quiltmaking.

EDITOR: TONI TOOMEY
COPY EDITOR: CHRYSTAL ABHALTER
GRAPHIC DESIGN: AMY CHASE
COVER DESIGN: MICHAEL BUCKINGHAM
QUILT PHOTOS: CHARLES R. LYNCH
HOW-TO PHOTOS: MARK J. WOOD

Library of Congress Cataloging-in-Publication Data

Wood, Julia C.
  Fabric photo play / by Julia C. Wood.
      p. cm.
   Summary: "Instructions for creating patterns from photos for use on wall quilts, jackets, pillows, and more"--Provided by publisher.
   ISBN 1-57432-879-4
   1. Quilts--Design. 2. Patchwork--Patterns.   3. Portrait photography. I. Title.

   TT835.W654 2005
   746.46'041--dc22

                                    2004029948

Additional copies of this book may be ordered from the American Quilter's Society, PO Box 3290, Paducah, KY 42002-3290, or call 1-800-626-5420 or online at www.AmericanQuilter.com.

Dedication

This is for my daughters, Emily and Elizabeth. May you both discover outlets in your lives that give you as much pleasure as quilting gives me. Here's to dreams coming true.

Acknowledgements

What a wonderful experience this project has been! My imagination has stretched along with my circle of friends. So many kind souls have supported me in this endeavor in a variety of ways, and words will never be able to express the gratitude I have. Nonetheless, I'll do my best to attempt a few heartfelt thanks:

Mark, my husband—As always, I give you my love and devotion; you've always supported my many projects without complaining about the piles of fabric covering every surface in our house.

Emily and Elizabeth, our daughters—I appreciate your support, excitement, and patience. And thanks for not complaining when I didn't have time to cook a decent dinner!

Dudley and Melba Cheape, my parents—Thank you for everything, from raising me well, to giving me the gifts of sewing and creativity. Thanks also for helping me with the last few quilts and helping me clean my house when the dust bunnies were out of control.

Clyde and Carolyn Wood, my in-laws—Thanks for all your support and encouragement and also for all those meals you cooked for us when my schedule was tight.

Birmingham Quilt Guild—I wouldn't be where I am without you. You all inspire me every month with your beautiful quilts and sunny personalities.

One Stitch Closer Bee—Your friendships have meant so much to me! Thanks for all your help in putting together samples for my book proposal.

Art Quilt Bee—Thanks for helping me think outside the box. You've helped me push my limits with art and with quilts.

Crosshaven Books Writers' Group—Wow, what an impact you've all had on me! You are all so talented and mean the world to me.

Joyce Cook—You are such a talented photographer. Thanks for allowing me to use some of your fabulous photographs for my quilts.

RJR Fabrics—Thanks for providing the beautiful Jinny Beyer fabric for my samples.

Karen Combs—Thanks for sending me your wonderful fabric for use in my samples.

The Warm Company—Thanks for the Steam-a-Seam 2®, my favorite fusible product.

Table of Contents

Introduction

For the past couple of centuries, quilting has been known as a craft, primarily a utilitarian craft. Making bedcovers from fabric scraps met a basic human need—staying warm at night. As quilting has experienced a resurgence during the past few decades, something wonderful has occurred. Quilters have pushed their limits, stretched their imaginations, and broken the rules, turning out quilted masterpieces, creations that would probably cause our quilting ancestors to drop their needles in amazement. Quilting is not just a craft anymore—it's a true art in every sense of the word.

I have been constantly amazed by the work some quilters achieve. A recent trip to the Museum of the American Quilter's Society opened my eyes even wider. For years I'd been studying quilt magazines and quilting books, watching my favorite quilting shows on television. But nothing prepared me for seeing such masterpieces in person. The workmanship was impeccable. The designs were beyond my imagination. It was like being a child surrounded by a roomful of candy and toys.

For a few years I've had the desire to make my own masterpiece. I wanted to steer away from the traditional pieced and appliquéd patterns. I wanted portraits of our children. So the idea crept into the back of my mind—maybe I could someday do quilt portraits.

I wanted to do portraits of our dogs, too. I knew there were quilting patterns of various breeds available on the market, but three out of five of our dogs are mixed breeds that we saved from the animal shelter. They are unique canines and no commercially available pattern looks like any of them.

Fabric Photo Play • Julia C. Wood

Then came my epiphany. One of our daughters brought a photograph of herself home from school. It had been taken as part of a school project. It wasn't special in any way, but as I looked at the photo, instead of seeing my daughter, I began to see areas of light and dark. The shadows in the photograph could be related to differences in light and dark fabrics. Suddenly I had an idea for duplicating the image using my quilting fabrics. Voilá! Shadow portraits!

I gave it a try, and much to my surprise, it worked. I was thrilled with how realistic my first shadow portrait turned out. Every new portrait that I tried was better than the last. And so was the beginning of my new quilting adventure.

In this book, I will show you how to get started making your own shadow portraits. You will learn to identify and use areas of light and dark in a photograph to pull out the essential, unique features that define a person's or pet's face. From there you will take a few easy steps toward completing your first shadow portrait. And your own adventure begins!

Supplies

Here's a list of the basic supplies you will need to make a portrait quilt:

- Photograph—You will need a clear headshot of a person or an animal.

- Tracing paper

- Pencil—A mechanical pencil holds its point well.

- Clear upholstery vinyl

- Black permanent marker

- Steam-a-Seam 2® fusible web

- Iron

- Scissors—Small, very sharp scissors work best for accurately cutting small pieces of fused fabric.

- Fabric—You will need a good assortment of values from very light to very dark. Avoid large prints, stripes, and plaids.

- Brayer—Rollers made of wood, rubber, or plastic, called brayers, are readily available in most craft stores or from www.rings-things.com.

- Optional—Photo editing software such as Microsoft® Picture It! Digital Image Pro. See pages 17–20 for tips on using software to simplify making your pattern.

Fabric Photo Play • Julia C. Wood

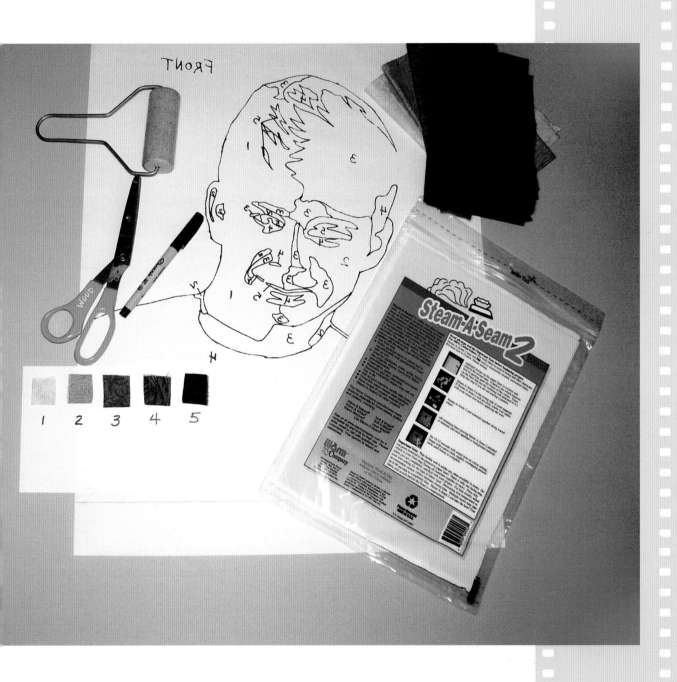

Making Your Pattern

PURPLE BOY
16"x 20". Made by the author.
Based on a photograph by Joyce Cook.

This is the third shadow portrait I've made from the photograph of a friend's son. Compare this quilt to BLUE BOY, pictured on page 50. As you can see, starting from two different patterns gave me two shadow portraits faithful to the original subject.

Tracing Values

A shadow portrait begins with a pattern made by tracing the different values in a photograph. This may seem difficult at first, but it's really only a matter of outlining areas of different values. You will need a photograph, a piece of tracing paper, and a mechanical pencil.

Value in Shadow Portraits

Value—the amount of light or dark visible in a color—is the key to success in shadow portraits. Figure 1 shows six values on a gray scale, and figure 2 shows six values of blue and yellow.

Fig. 1. Six values from black to white.

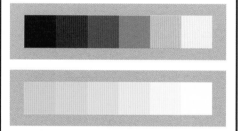

Fig. 2. Six values of dark blue to pale blue and dark yellow to pale yellow.

It's the shifts in value in a black-and-white photo that make a face recognizable. A lot of different values are not necessary. As you can see in figure 3, even though the portraits are rendered with only two values, the faces are still recognizable.

Fig. 3. Portraits in two values are unmistakable.

1 It's easier to see the values in a black-and-white image, especially when it is enlarged. Make a photocopy of your original photo, enlarged to 8" x 10". (You can also do this on a scanner.) Lay a piece of tracing paper over the enlarged photocopy (fig. 4).

Fig. 4. Lay tracing paper over the enlarged photo.

2 Using a pencil, trace the outline of the head and shoulders of the subject (fig. 5). (Think in terms of a silhouette.) Keep in mind that when you get to the shoulders, your drawing does not have to be literal.

TIP

For your first shadow portrait, you may find it difficult to ignore the facial features. Try tracing the photo upside down, so you can ignore the facial features and simply concentrate on the values.

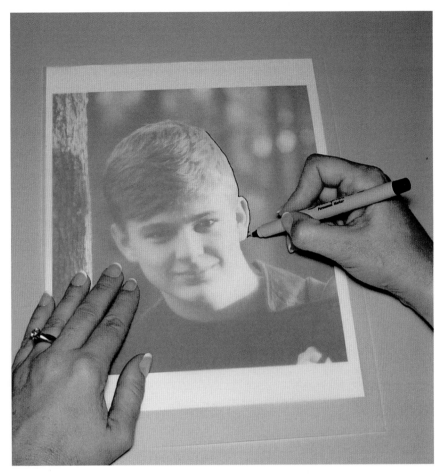

Fig. 5. Trace around the head and shoulders.

3 Study the variations in value and trace what you see. Look for large areas of different values. At first, focus only on three values—dark, medium, and light (fig. 6, page 14). Later you may isolate one or two more values that add detail to your tracing. But even with only three values, a realistic likeness of the subject will emerge. Make sure each traced area is enclosed, so that it can be cut out of fabric later.

Remember, there are no right or wrong places to draw the changes in value. Two people could use the same photo and draw two extremely different patterns, but both would end up with successful shadow portraits. Draw the way you, the artist, see the values.

Fig. 6. Outline the main areas of dark, medium, and light values.

4 Once you've outlined your three main value areas, remove the tracing paper from the photocopy and study your drawing. You will add detail in the next steps, but for now, if the portrait is recognizable, you're on the right track.

Fig. 7. Label the outlined areas with "1," "2," and "3".

5 When you are satisfied with your outlines, label the lightest areas "1," the medium areas "2," and the darkest areas "3" (fig. 7). I used permanent marker for the figures in this chapter so my outlines would show up clearly. But you might want to continue working in pencil until your pattern is finished.

6 Start looking for smaller areas that will add detail to your shadow portrait. In this step, you can outline value difference within the larger areas you outlined in step 3.

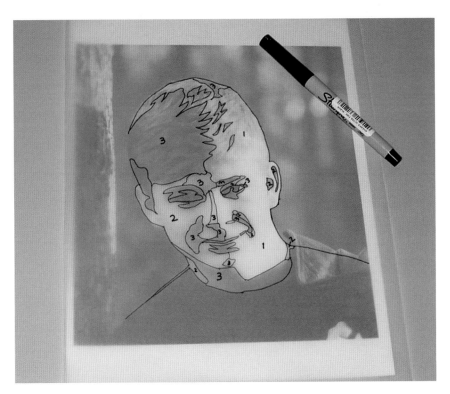

Fig. 8. Outline details to bring out the subject's features.

7 Focus on the important areas of the photo such as the facial features. By simply tracing around a few different values, the details of the subject's features will appear as if by magic in the final portrait (fig. 8).

Avoid the temptation to draw the eyes, the nose, and the mouth in detail. Keep it simple. Don't go overboard delineating too many tiny spots of varying value. Remember, each different area will have to be cut out of fabric eventually.

8 Once again, remove the tracing paper from the photocopy and study your drawing. Are the main facial features identifiable? Is the portrait recognizable? If so, you're done! If it seems to be missing something—maybe the nose doesn't look quite right—adjust your drawing, tracing as necessary. Erase lines and redraw new ones as needed until you are satisfied with the pattern.

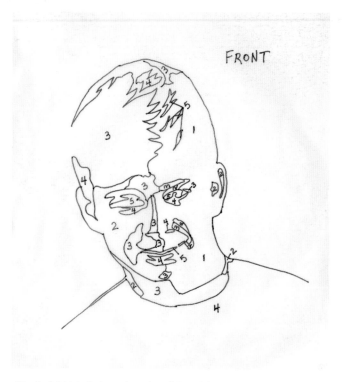

Fig. 9. Add labels for values 4 and 5 and the word "front."

9 Label the new value areas you outlined. These areas should be darker than the first three values. Start with the darkest areas and label them "5." Then label the remaining areas "4." These numbers will coincide with the fabrics you will select in the next chapter.

Limit Your Values

Students often ask how many values they should label. I've done quilts with as few as one value all the way up to six or seven different values. For your first project, I suggest limiting yourself to three or four different values, plus the background.

10 With a permanent marker, write the word "front" prominently at the top of your pattern (fig. 9). Then draw over your pencil tracing and labels with the permanent marker.

Letting Your Computer Do the Walking

The main challenge in making patterns for shadow portraits is looking at a photograph with so many different values and "seeing" only four or five. I have found that photo-imaging software programs now available can make this task a lot easier. I can get a good pattern using either method—tracing by hand, or generating computerized patterns. The main difference is the speed and convenience of letting my computer do some of the work.

You can use any rudimentary photo-imaging software program that comes free with your digital camera or your scanner to make similar adjustments to a photo. You can also purchase inexpensive software, such as Microsoft® Picture It! Digital Image Pro 7.0, for making your patterns. I used some of the advanced features in Picture It! to show you how I use photo imaging to help make patterns for my shadow portraits.

1 Whether you trace by hand or use computer imaging to create a pattern for a shadow portrait, you need to start with a clear photograph with good shadows. Upload the photo to the computer. There are three ways to do this:

—If the photo was taken with a digital camera, upload the photo to the computer according to the camera instructions.

—If the photo was taken with a 35mm camera, request a photo CD when the film is developed. You can then upload your photos from the CD to your computer.

—If the photo was taken with a 35mm camera and a photo CD is not available, use a flat bed scanner to scan the photo to the computer. Try making the following adjustments both before and after scanning the photo.

2 Once the photo is uploaded to the computer, start your photo-editing program.

3 Click File>Open, and select the file containing your photo. The photograph will appear on the screen (fig. 10). Save a copy of the photo with a different file name. Don't change the original photo, because once you have saved changes to your original photo, there's no going back.

Fig. 10. Open a photograph in your photo-editing program.

4 If you are using a color photograph, regardless of the software you are using, you first need to use your software's color adjustments to remove all of the color from (or desaturate) the image.

5 Select your software's sharpening option and sharpen the image's focus to the maximum possible (fig. 11). With the software that comes with your scanner or digital camera you can now decrease the brightness of your photo and increase the contrast. This will remove most of the value variations in your photo and make it easier to select and trace the values for your shadow portrait.

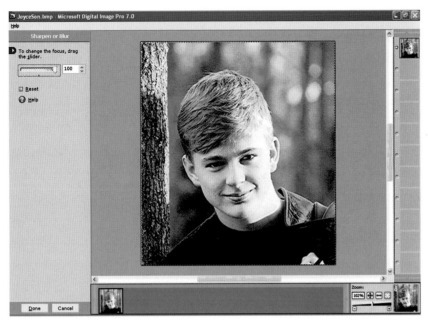

Fig. 11. Sharpen the focus of the image to the maximum possible.

6 My Picture It! software lets me go a step further: Click on the Effects icon on the left side of the screen (a red and green apple) and select Filters from the menu that appears. In the Filters menu, select the Cutout filter. This filter converts the photo into different value areas (fig. 12).

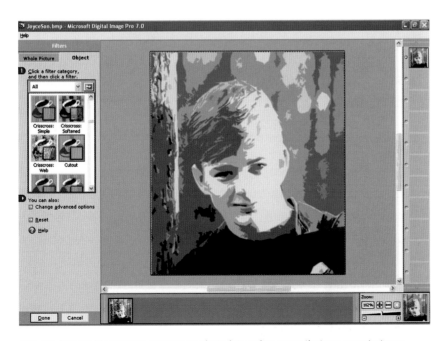

Fig. 12. Picture It! program converts a photo into value areas that are easy to trace.

7 If the image is identifiable as the subject and you are satisfied at this point, simply print the image. The image in figure 12 would work well for a pattern, however I'd like to get more detail on the right side of his mouth. I can do this by tweaking the brightness and contrast.

8 In Picture It! you can cancel the changes you've made so far and try to improve the pattern by adjusting the brightness and contrast. This part of the process is trial and error. At this point, I try different settings for the brightness and contrast and test them by applying the Cutout filter each time until I'm satisfied with the pattern. Figure 13 shows another version of a pattern from the same original photo.

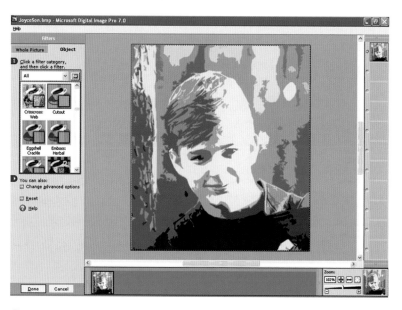

Fig. 13. Different adjustments will give you a slightly different pattern.

9 When you're satisfied that your image will make a good pattern for a shadow portrait, make an 8½" x 11" print out of it. Now you can proceed with tracing your image and making your pattern, as explained in pages 11–16.

I have found that I can get a good pattern using either method—tracing by hand, or generating computerized patterns. The main difference is the speed and convenience of letting my computer do some of the work.

Finishing Your Pattern

Next you will need to visit a copy center to enlarge your traced pattern. We began by tracing the values in an 8" x 10" photocopy of your portrait because that seems to be the ideal size for distinguishing the values in the photo.

The size of the copy you make will depend on how big you want your quilt to be. The finished portrait will be the exact size of the pattern you use. I use a copy center that has the capacity to make oversized copies, up to 36" x 36". I usually start with enlarging it 200%. Sometimes I go bigger, up to 400% larger than the original. I'm partial to large oversized images, but you may prefer a smaller portrait quilt. The bigger the quilt is, the less intricate the pieces will be.

You will use this enlarged photocopy when you cut the fabric for your shadow portrait. But first, you will make a vinyl overlay that will be essential for positioning fabric pieces in the correct places. I use clear upholstery vinyl for this. It's widely available in fabric stores in sixty-inch width. Any weight of vinyl will work.

1 The copy of your traced pattern needs to be the reverse image of your original photograph (fig. 14). Make sure to place your traced pattern in the copier "front" side up. The lines and labels drawn in permanent marker will show through the tracing paper to give you the reverse image you need.

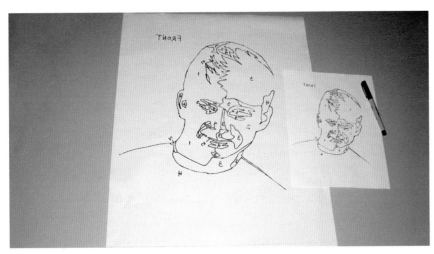

Fig. 14. Make an enlarged, reverse-image photocopy of your traced pattern.

2 Cut a piece of vinyl the same size as the enlarged, photocopied pattern. Lay the vinyl over the photocopy and trace the entire pattern with a permanent marker (fig. 15). It is not necessary to include the value labels in this vinyl overlay.

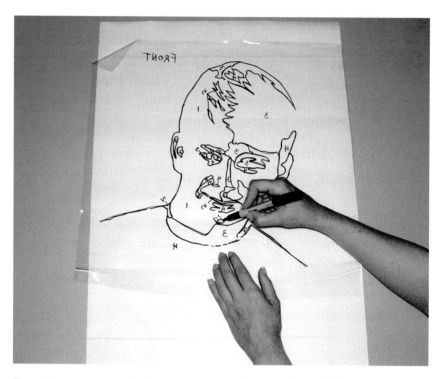

Fig. 15. Trace the enlarged photocopy onto a sheet of upholstery vinyl.

Now that you have a photocopy of your pattern and a copy of it drawn on vinyl, you are ready to select your fabric and assemble your shadow portrait.

Making Your Shadow Portrait

Selecting Fabrics

With a pattern based on a range of values in your original photograph, it's time to select fabrics based on that same range of values.

It may seem odd to make a portrait from monochromatic fabric. For most of my shadow portraits I use five or six fabrics in different values from one color family. Pick any color you wish, black, red, purple, green, blue—it doesn't matter. Many people cringe when I tell them they can do a portrait in a color like purple. "But my granddaughter doesn't have purple hair!" Don't worry! I promise you'll get dramatic results.

FAQ

Q: Can I get enough different values for a shadow portrait if I want to use a light color family?

A: Yes you can, even though you may not get as much contrast between the values. Referring to the example of values of blue and yellow in figure 16, if it looks to you like the range of values—or the amount of contrast—in the family of yellows is less than the contrast in the family of blues, you're right. However, both light and dark color families make good shadow quilts. Compare RYAN (pictured on page 45) and TEDDY (pictured on page 61) to see how the color family you pick determines the overall effect of the quilt.

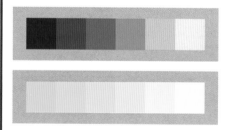

Fig. 16. While there is more contrast in the family of blues, there is enough contrast in the family of yellows to make a shadow portrait.

I have my fabric stash sorted by color in wire basket drawers, which makes this step simple. I prefer not to work with solid fabric, but I don't like big, busy prints either. I like to use fabrics with small prints with good texture that read as solid from a distance.

1 Select ten to fifteen fabrics in one color family that vary in value from very light to very dark. Lay them on a work surface in order from light to dark so that about the same amount of each fabric is visible (fig. 17).

Fig. 17. Select ten to fifteen fabrics from the same color family in a range of values.

2 You will select one fabric for each value in your pattern. In the case of the shadow portrait of the boy, I traced and labeled five values, so I need to select five fabrics. (We'll get to the background fabric in a minute.)

3 Pick a fabric very near the left end for the lightest value in the quilt (fabric number 1). Pick a fabric very near the right end for the darkest value for the background in the quilt (in this quilt, fabric number 5, as shown in figure 18).

4 For fabric number 3, pick a fabric with a value somewhere in the middle between fabrics 1 and 5 (fig. 19). As you can see, from this point on your selections will be made according to your own eye and what looks good to you. Just as there were no right or wrong answers when you chose the values to trace in your patterns, there are no right or wrong answers to deciding which fabrics to select. In other words, trust your eye.

Fig. 18. Pick your lightest and darkest fabrics for values 1 and 5.

Fig. 19. Select a value between fabrics 1 and 5.

5 For your fabric number 2, pick a fabric between 1 and 3. This fabric needs to vary distinctly in value from 1 and 3. Pick a fabric between 3 and 5 to serve as fabric number 4, again one that is distinct in value from 3 and 5 (figure 20, page 26).

Fig. 20. For values 2 and 4, select two more fabrics distinctly different in values from the others.

6 Pull out your final selections, and glue or tape a small swatch of each fabric to an index card and label the fabrics 1 though 5 (or however many values you have selected). This card will serve as a key to fabric placement throughout the process (fig. 21).

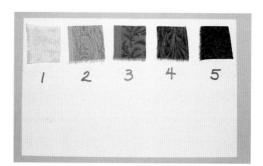

Fig. 21. Five fabrics for values 1–5 are selected from one color family. Label a swatch of each fabric on an index card.

After you have made your fabric selections for the shadow portrait, you will pick a background fabric. To do this, first examine the pattern, looking at the pattern numbers that appear around the edges of the of the subject's hair, face, and shoulders. The goal is to select a background fabric that will contrast with the fabrics around these edges.

For example, if the subject's hair is a dark value, you wouldn't want it to be next to a dark background. If most of the portrait edge pieces are dark, choose a light or medium background fabric. If the edge pieces are mostly light, choose a medium or dark background fabric. If the perimeter pieces are mostly medium, choose a light or dark background fabric. Pull the background fabric from the remaining fabrics in your color family. In fact, as long as it's a different value from the ones around the edges, the background fabric can even be the same as one used in the portrait.

As a rule, I select a background fabric that contrasts with the edges of the shadow portrait. However, if you look at BLUE BOY, pictured on page 50, you will notice that I did use one of the portrait fabrics for my background. But the fabric (value 3) does not contrast with all of the portrait edges. As you can see in the quilt, the left side of the boy's hair is the same value and the same fabric as the background. This was a judgment call that I let my eye determine. When you select your background fabric, start with my rule of thumb outlined above, then feel free to break the rule according to what looks good to you.

FAQ

Q: Should I use 100 percent cotton fabric?

A: Not necessarily. I work mostly in cotton fabric. But I've also had great success with cotton blends and even with dupioni silk. Choose a fabric that can handle a hot iron and can easily be quilted through.

FAQ

Q: Should I prewash my fabric?

A: I'm not a prewasher, though I know some quilters feel they must wash all fabric before they use it. I look at these portrait quilts as art that will be hung on a wall. I don't intend to ever wash them, so I don't worry about the possibility of dyes running or fabrics shrinking. But it certainly won't hurt to prewash the fabric.

A Word About Fusible Web

Fusible web is the key to quickly creating shadow portrait quilts. After experimenting with various brands, I've come to the conclusion that Steam-a-Seam 2® is the best option for me. It is easy to machine quilt through and maintains a softness suitable for a quilt. However, its tacky surface is the best characteristic of Steam-a-Seam 2® for making shadow portraits. I can put a piece of fabric backed with Steam-a-Seam 2® in place on my background and it will stay put even before I iron it in place permanently. With other fusible web products, I must iron after positioning each and every piece, otherwise they can slide out of place.

Putting the Pieces Together

Now that the preliminary work is complete, the real fun begins as we watch the shadow portrait come to life before our eyes. It's best to work on a large work surface with enough room for the portrait to lay flat, along with space for the fusible web, fabric, scissors, and pattern close at hand. Have a small trash can handy for discarding scraps of fabric and fusible web.

1 Press the background fabric, and place it right-side up on a smooth work surface. Anchor the fabric at the top, bottom, and both sides with a few pieces of masking tape.

2 Place the vinyl overlay on top of the background fabric. Be sure to position the vinyl overlay so it's going in the same direction as your original photograph. Tape the vinyl overlay in place at the top only (fig. 22).

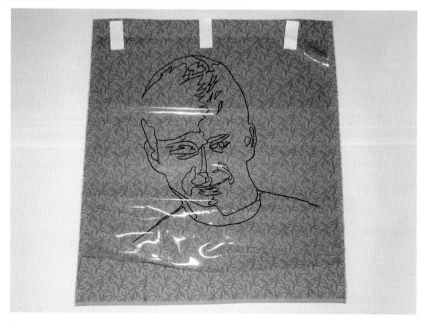

Fig. 22. Tape a vinyl overlay in place over background fabric.

3 Take a piece of Steam-a-Steam 2 and separate it just a bit at one corner. The fusible web is sandwiched between two pieces of paper. The web generally wants to stick to one of the paper pieces more than the other one. You will trace each pattern piece with pencil or pen on the side of the Steam-a-Steam 2 that does not pull away from the webbing easily. Place a small *x* on the corner of the fusible web to indicate on which side to do the tracing.

4 Study the enlarged pattern to find the largest pieces with which to begin. Remember, you are now working with the reverse-image photocopy of your pattern (with "front" appearing backwards). Trace the largest piece onto the fusible web, as in figure 23. Starting with the larger pieces will minimize the intricate cutting later.

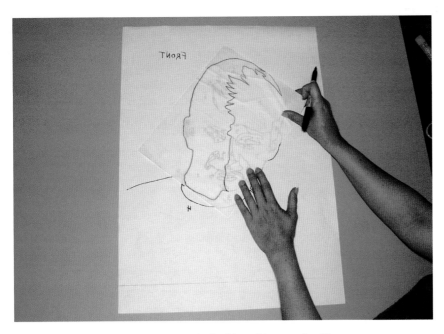

Fig. 23. Trace a numbered piece onto the fusible web's paper backing.

5 Write the value number on the tracing, and add a short description of where the piece will be placed, such as "left eye" or "neck."

6 Peel the paper from the back of the fusible web (not the traced side). Be careful to make sure that the fusible web layer stays with the traced paper. Place the traced pattern piece on the wrong side of the correct valued fabric (fig. 24). In other words, if the pattern piece is labeled "2," place it on the wrong side of fabric number 2. For smaller pieces, roughly cut around the traced image (at least ½" outside the traced line) before sticking it to the wrong side of the appropriate fabric.

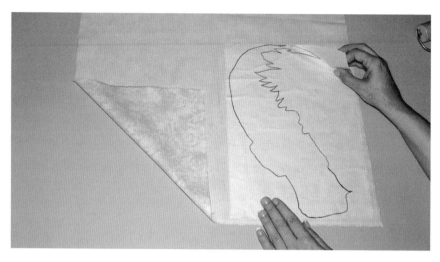

Fig. 24. Place fusible web against the wrong side of the fabric.

7 Use a brayer or the edge of a credit card to smooth the pattern onto the fabric for maximum adhesion. Do not iron the pattern to the fabric at this point.

8 Cut out the fabric along the traced lines, as shown in figure 25. Use small scissors when necessary to cut small details.

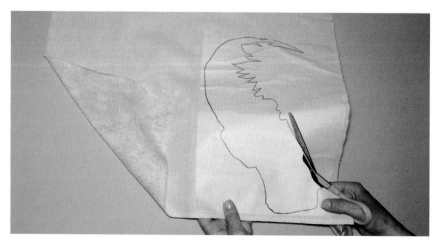

Fig. 25. Cut out fabric along the traced pattern line.

9 Remove the paper from the fabric, making sure the fusible layer stays with the fabric. Gently lift the vinyl overlay and position the fabric, fusible side down, making sure it is aligned in the correct position according to the vinyl overlay, (fig. 26).

10 Lower the overlay to check the position of the fabric piece. Adjust the piece until it is properly aligned with the overlay, as in figure 27.

11 Replace the vinyl overlay. Use a brayer or credit card to firmly press the fabric against the background (fig. 28, page 32).

Note: Do not iron at this point. The portrait will not be permanently fused in place with a hot iron until every piece is satisfactorily in place at the end.

> **TIP**
> For best results, rotate the fabric while cutting, keeping the scissors in the same position.

> **TIP**
> You will not do any pressing until all of your fabric pieces are in place in your shadow portrait. However, as you work, the Steam-a-Seam may want to pull away from the fabric. Secure it back in place by firmly rolling a brayer over the webbing.

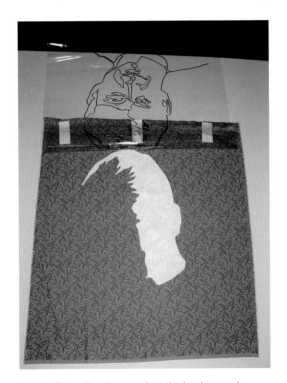

Fig. 26. Place the piece against the background.

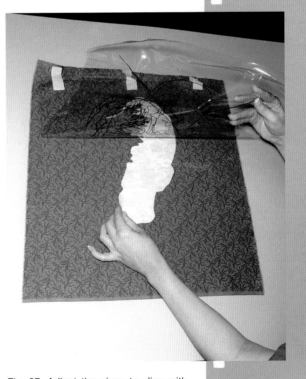

Fig. 27. Adjust the piece to align with the outline on the overlay.

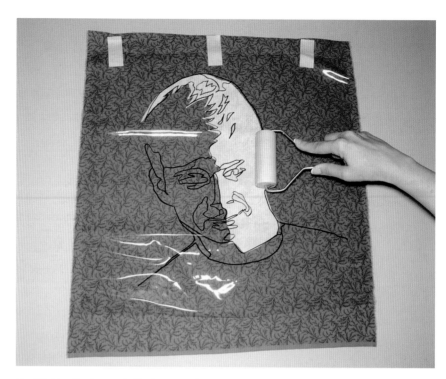

Fig. 28. Use the brayer to firmly press the fabric piece to the background.

12 Proceed by adding the other larger pieces to the background, as in figure 29.

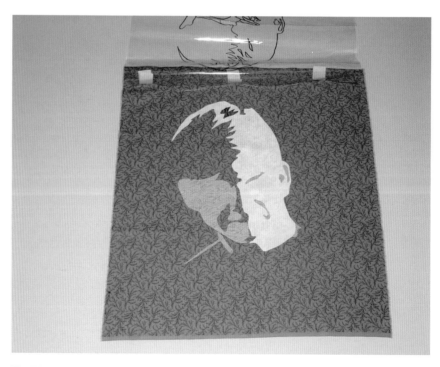

Fig. 29. Add large pieces to the background before placing smaller pieces.

13 Continue in the same manner, tracing each pattern piece, adhering it to the wrong side of the correct fabric, cutting the piece from the fabric, and positioning it on the shadow portrait background. Be sure to work from the larger pieces to the smaller pieces, layering the pieces as needed. Notice that the background in figure 30 is left exposed where the value-3 pieces would be placed.

Fig. 30. Check that pieces are correctly placed and that the shadow image seems complete.

Finishing Your Shadow Portrait Quilt

Once all the pieces are in place, it is time to permanently fuse the portrait using a hot iron. Do not iron until all pieces are satisfactorily in place. This allows for changing a fabric late into the process if needed. The Steam-a-Seam's tackiness keeps the pieces in place temporarily.

1 Remove the vinyl overlay from the background fabric. Using a hot iron with no steam, press in an up-and-down motion, making sure every small piece is adhered. Do not slide the iron over the surface, as this may cause small pieces to be slid out of place (fig. 31).

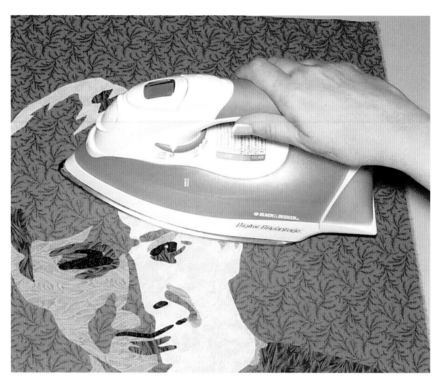

Fig. 31. Press with a gentle up-and-down motion to keep the small pieces in place.

2 When I finish assembling a shadow portrait, I decide if it needs a border. Some faces fill the background space so well that no border seems to be necessary. But some portraits seem to float in space and need a simple border to appropriately frame them. Keep borders for shadow portrait quilts simple. Too much intricate piecing, such as flying geese or other patterns with lots of motion, will draw attention away from the portrait.

3 Once all the pieces of the shadow portrait have been positioned and fused in place, it can be turned into a quilted wallhanging. Cut a piece of cotton batting that is a few inches larger than the shadow portrait. Cut a piece of backing fabric that is approximately the same size as the batting.

4 Place the backing fabric right side down on a smooth surface. Tape the edges of the backing to the surface, making sure the backing is taut without being stretched.

5 Place the batting over the backing fabric. Smooth and tape in place. Then place the shadow portrait over the batting, again smoothing and taping the edges.

6 Using small (no.1) safety pins, baste the three layers together. Pins should be spaced approximately three inches apart.

7 If you've never tried machine quilting, this is the perfect opportunity to try "scribbling" with your sewing machine. The stitching lines don't have to be a certain distance apart, and it's fine to cross over our quilting seams. It's the best way to make sure all the shadow portrait pieces are sufficiently tacked down. Plus, there's no way to make a mistake.

8 Another great technique for machine quilting portraits is "sketching." Use the quilting to sketch rough lines that emphasize the hair and the curvature of the face.

9 Once the quilting is finished, add binding to finish off the edges.

Tips on Machine Quilting

1 Work with the feed dogs lowered or covered.

2 Use a darning foot or free-motion quilting foot.

3 Use gloves designed for machine quilting so the quilt will not slip beneath your fingers.

4 Use a separate thread stand for the spool so that thread will feed into the machine from above.

5 If your machine has a needle-down function, be sure to use it at all times.

These tips should help a beginning machine quilter have success. Before quilting a shadow portrait, it's always a good idea to practice on a small quilt. I keep a practice sandwich (made with two scraps of muslin filled with a scrap of cotton batting) handy beside my machine.

The most important factor in machine quilting is *relax*! Remember, you cannot make a mistake. Turn up your radio and go with the flow. Free yourself to let loose, making smooth curves, squiggles, and loops.

Projects

Portrait Purse

OLIVER PURSE
12" x 14". Made by the author.
Based on a photograph by Julia Wood, page 56.

This quilt was so tiny, that I decided to make a purse from it. I used all polka-dot fabrics.

Shadow portrait.............................no larger than 13" x 13"
Fabric for purse back..1 fat quarter
Fabric for purse side......................................4" x 36" strip
Fabric for lining...¾ yd.
Fabric for binding ....3" x 34" strip
Cotton batting ....two 15" squares
Timtex® interfacing
Purse pattern (page 39)
Magnetic purse closure
Purse handle

Making the Outer Purse

1 If your shadow portrait is smaller than 13" x 13", sew strips of coordinating fabric around each side until it measures at least 13" x 13".

2 Layer a 15" x 15" square of Timtex® interfacing with a 15" x 15" square of cotton batting and the fabric portrait. Pin these layers together in several places.

3 Quilt the layers by "scribbling," making sure to stitch over each individual piece of fabric in the portrait. While quilting, hold onto the quilt with the extra Timtex® around the edges. A new, sharp quilting needle will make this easier.

4 Layer a 15" x 15" piece of Timtex® with a 15" x 15" square of cotton batting and your purse backing fabric. Pin and scribble quilt the layers.

5 Enlarge the purse pattern (page 39) 200 percent. Use the pattern to cut one purse front from the shadow portrait and one purse back.

6 Cut a piece of 4" x 36" strip of Timtex® and layer it with your 4" x 36" strip of coordinating fabric. Sew the layers every few inches across the width to secure the two layers together.

7 Mark the center bottom of the purse front (shadow portrait) and the purse back with a pin. Mark the center of the 36" strip with a pin on either side.

8 Matching centers, pin the purse front to the 36" strip, fabric sides together. Clip the 36" strip in the area where it will be joined with the curved edges on the purse. Sew using a ⅜" seam from the left center bottom, around the curve, and to the left top. Repeat, sewing from the right center bottom to the right top.

9 Sew the back of the purse to the 4" x 36" strip in the same manner, sewing from the center bottom up one side and repeating for the other side.

10 Trim the top edges of the purse so they are even.

Lining and Finishing Your Purse

1 Cut a purse front and back, along with a 4" x 36" strip from your lining fabric. Sew these pieces together in the same manner as the outer purse.

2 Place the lining inside the purse, wrong sides together. Pin in place around the top edges.

3 Cut a piece of 3" x 34" binding from coordinating fabric. Fold the binding in half lengthwise, wrong sides together, and press.

4 Pin the binding around the outside purse top, lining up the raw edges, and pinning through the binding, outer purse, and lining layers. Machine stitch the binding to the purse using a ⅜" seam allowance.

5 Insert the magnet purse closure pieces through the binding on the center of each side of the purse.

6 Fold the binding to the inside of the purse and hand stitch in place.

7 Center the handles on each side of the purse and secure with pliers.

PRINCE PURSE
Made by the author.
Based on a photograph by Julia Wood.

Purse Pattern

Enlarge 200%

Portrait Pillows

ROSIE PILLOW & MAGGIE PILLOW

ROSIE PILLOW
10" x 25". Made by the author.
Based on a photograph by Julia Wood.

Family pets are a big favorite for my portrait quilts. Rosie is my brother-in-law's dog.

MAGGIE PILLOW
10" x 25". Made by the author.
Based on a photograph by Julia Wood.

My mother-in-law's Maggie looks as good in fabric as she does in beads.

MAGGIE IN BEADS

MAGGIE IN BEADS
20" x 20". Made by the author.
Based on a photograph by Julia Wood.

I used the same portrait pattern as I
did for the MAGGIE PILLOW. But instead
of using fabric, I hand stitched beads
to a black background.

Detail, MAGGIE PILLOW

This pillow used the same portrait pattern as the other Maggie pillow. Your shadow portrait can adorn a wall, or you can turn it into a cozy. Once you have your portrait pattern, think about other ways to create the portrait—with beads, for example. These pillows make fabulous gifts!

Detail, MAGGIE IN BEADS

```
┌─────────────────────────────────────────────┐
│ To make a portrait pillow, you will need:    │
│                                              │
│     • Shadow portrait                        │
│     • Assorted fabrics                       │
│       (upholstery/drapery fabric work fine)  │
│     • Assorted trims                         │
│     • Polyester pillow stuffing              │
└─────────────────────────────────────────────┘
```

A pillow is bound to get a lot more of wear and tear than a wall-hanging. To keep fused edges in the portrait from fraying, make sure it is thoroughly quilted.

1. Sew fabric strips to the edges of the shadow portrait until the pillow is the desired size.

2. Pin and sew trim to the right side edges of the pillow top.

3. Cut a back to the pillow the same size as the front.

4. Place the pillow top and backing right sides together.

5. Stitch around the pillow, leaving a small opening for turning and stuffing.

6. Turn the pillow right side out. Stuff the pillow, then hand stitch the opening closed.

MADDIE

MADDIE
24½" x 25½". Made by the author and Rebecca Langston.
Based on a photograph by Phillip Dupree.

The Four-Patch border is a whimsical
addition to this sweet dog.

RYAN
26" x 21". Made by the author.
Based on a photograph by John Cheape.

I took a different approach in this quilt of my nephew,
using conversational prints. In some ways, it's busy
and distracts from the quality of the portrait, but it is a
fun exercise and does bring out Ryan's personality.

CIGARETTE MAN

Photograph by Joyce Cook.

CIGARETTE MAN
20" x 13". Made by the author.

This graphic quilt was based on a photo
by Joyce Cook of her oldest son.

BOY WITH FISH
10" x 13". Made by the author and Jeanette Prestel.
Based on a photograph by Jeanette Prestel.

In the original photo, James was holding a
bird feeder. I replaced it with the gold fish.

HAIRDRESSER
32" x 31". Made by the author.
Based on a photograph by Julia Wood.

Tim Mayo is my hair stylist. This fun quilt lets his personality shine through. The comb in his hand is a real plastic comb that is hand stitched to the quilt. The hair from his hand is cut from a wig, adding dimension to the flat surface.

BLUE BOY
19" x 15". Made by the author.

This is the first in a series of quilts
based on the same photograph taken
by Joyce Cook of her son.

MICHAEL
17½" x 19". Pattern by the author and assembled by Rebecca Langston.
Based on a photograph by Phillip Dupree.

The light background in this quilt is balanced
by the dark border. The combination brings
the eye straight to Michael's smile.

DANGLING FEET

Photograph by Joyce Cook.

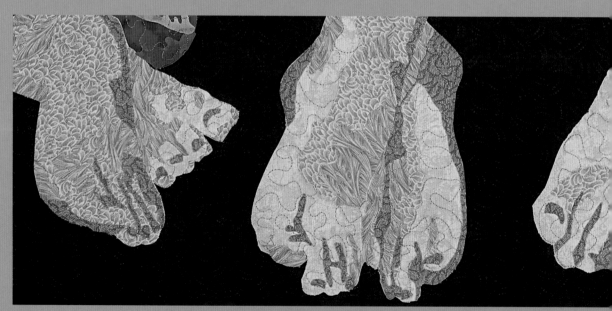

Detail, DANGLING FEET

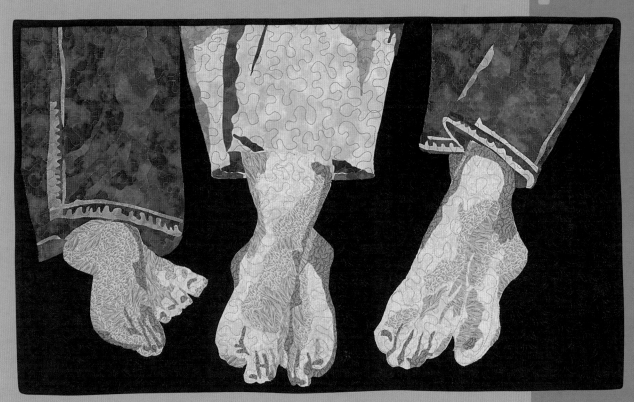

DANGLING FEET
18" x 30". Made by the author.

CHAMPIONS

CHAMPIONS
23" x 26". Made by the author.

Marion Brakefield and her champion horse.

CHRISTA AND MICHAEL
20½" x 17½". Assembled by Rebecca Langston.
Pattern and quilting by the author.
Based on a photograph by Phillip Dupree.

Rebecca, a good friend, made
this quilt of her grandchildren.

OLIVER II

Photograph by Julia Wood.

OLIVER II
30" x 14". Made by the author.

INNOCENCE
25" x 36". Made by the author.
Based on a photograph by Ngozi Asinga.

SHARON'S WEDDING DAY

SHARON'S WEDDING DAY
19" x 20½". Made by the author and Rebecca Langston.
Based on a photograph by Rebecca Langston.

TEDDY

Photograph by Julia Wood.

TEDDY
13" x 11". Made by the author.

This project was a study in value and color.
I used only three values. The medium value
is the background, but also reappears in
the dog's face. The asymmetrical borders
give the quilt a contemporary look.

FLOATING

About the Author

Julia Wood started sewing as a child, but her life took a more technical route during her career as an engineer. When she stopped working to stay home with her children, Julia returned to her creative roots and began quilting. Her love of computers and quilting led to the development of her technique to create shadow portraits of people and pets.

When not quilting or teaching about quilting, Julia enjoys entering cooking contests—she's been a two-time finalist in the Pillsbury Bake-Off®. She lives in Birmingham, Alabama, with her husband, Mark, their two daughters, Emily and Elizabeth, and their five dogs.

Other AQS Books

This is only a small selection of the books available from the American Quilter's Society. AQS books are known worldwide for timely topics, clear writing, beautiful color photos, and accurate illustrations and patterns. The following books are available from your local bookseller, quilt shop, or public library.

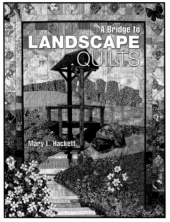

#6514   us$21.95

#6418   us$18.95

#6295   us$24.95

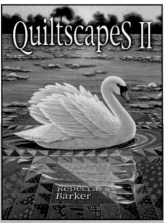

#6680   us$21.95

#6413   us$21.95

#6511   us$22.95

#6206   us$19.95

#6213   us$24.95

#6002   us$15.95

LOOK for these books nationally. **CALL** 1-800-626-5420
or **VISIT** our Web site at www.AmericanQuilter.com